POEMS ABOUT
WISDOM

By

Suru Ayo

ISBN: 978-969-2992-91-6

Table Of Contents

Foreword

One of the best things about wisdom is that it never goes out of fashion.

Just as old books are constantly being reopened and read, new insights about wisdom will always be being added.

Wisdom is timeless and its lessons can be applied to any situation or moment in life.

The more we learn and grow, the more we can see the value in wisdom.

It is an invaluable asset that can help us make the right decisions.

1

One day I will understand wisdom,

And all the things I know will suddenly make sense.

I won't be scared anymore

When in the dark I can't find my way.

I'll be brave when no one is around

And know that I am loved.

I'll be calm when the world is crazy

And know that I am in control.

I'll be kind when I can be mean

And know that.

2

She wears a face that hides her pain,

an icy fortress that protects her heart.

But on rare occasions, when the curtains fall ਏ

and the moonlight spills in like a tear,

she lets us glimpse the wisdom inside her eyes.

There are no secrets anymore,

only memories and lessons learned the hard way.

She's wisdom incarnate, and we would be lost.

3

What a deep and perfect gift,

Wisdom is.

What a precious treasure,

To keep and pass down through the years.

It is something to be cherished,

Not only by the wise,

But by all who know

The importance of learning,

And understanding.

4

———— ❧ ————

There she sits, veiled in thought,

learning and growing in wisdom daily

A wise owl is she, and she has seen

much in life, and now she seeks to impart

her knowledge to those around her.

She is patient, and never holds a grudge,

for she knows that wisdom is earned and not given.

She is kind, and always willing to lend

her help and advice to those who seek it.

5

Wisdom is an attribute we cannot live without

And it comes in different forms and sizes

Some have a lot of it, while others can barely scraps

But the most important thing is that everyone has

some

Wisdom is knowing what to do, and when to do it

It's being prudent, knowing when to speak, and when

to stay quiet

Wisdom is being kind and compassionate, and

forgiving

It's knowing when to stand up.

6

Age does not diminish wisdom,

nor does experience make it grow old.

Rather, it is the accumulation of understanding

that leads to years of experience.

wise words never expire.

7

❦

The wisdom that we've gained throughout our lives,

Has taught us how to navigate the treacherous seas,

And has helped us face the challenges that life throws

our way.

It has given us the knowledge to make the right

choices,

And it has shown us the way to live a happy life.

And I believe that wisdom is something that we

should always cherish,

For it is something that will always guide us in the

right direction.

8

I have often thought about wisdom,

And how it could fill up a big world,

And how everyone could be a wise one,

If only they would learn from their mistakes.

Wisdom is something that you need,

It can keep you out of trouble,

If you just find a way to use it.

Wisdom is a power that you can use,

It can show you the right way to go.

9

Wisdom is the source

From which all life derives

From the waters

To grow the trees

To the sun

Into the moon

Creating everything

We must remember

That wisdom is the key

To unlock the door

To find our way

And to be happy

It's the light

That guides our way.

10

What is wisdom?

A word without a definition

Something we all seek

A guide through life

A light in the dark

Wisdom is understanding

Knowing what is right and what is wrong

Carrying yourself with grace

Balance in times of chaos

Seeing beyond the surface

Knowing your own limitations

Wisdom is the key to a successful life

A path to happiness

A way to be content

A guide through life

A light in the dark.

11

With age comes wisdom,

And many a lesson learned,

Which oftentimes we might

Have otherwise gone without.

Wisdom to know when to speak,

And when to keep quiet;

To know that silence is golden,

And words seldom empower.

To know when to fight,

And when to run away;

To know the importance of making friends,

And never taking them for granted.

12

Wisdom is a deep insight that comes with years of experience.

It is knowing what to do, when to do it, and how to do it.

It is the ability to think outside the box, and see things in a different perspective.

It is the ability to see the big picture and make the right decisions.

Wisdom is knowing when to hold back, and when to take a chance.

It is the.

13

People may ask what wisdom is,

But I'll tell you what I know—

It's the ability to see things clearly

And make the right decisions.

It's the power to understand

And the know-how to guide your path.

Wisdom is knowing what's right

And doing what's best for yourself.

So, if you're looking for something

To help you on your way,

I suggest.

14

∼⧖∼

The wisdom of age is something we never outgrow

It's a natural thing that grows with time

It's something we all need, if we want to survive

The wisdom of age is something we never outgrow

It's a natural thing that grows with time

It's something we all need, if we want to survive

The older we get, the more we realize

That the world is a lot more complicated than we thought.

15

$$\sim\!\!\infty\!\!\sim$$

Wisdom is the secret of a long life

Better counsels than gold or silver

May bring you happiness from above.

16

What is wisdom?

A river of pure gold

A never ending message

That can guide us to the right path

A guide that never ends.

17

Tell me, O wisdom,

How to find the right path

When there are so many

And it seems so hard to know which one to take.

And tell me, O wisdom,

How to make the right choices

When it seems like every choice

Has its own set of consequences.

And tell me, O wisdom,

How to overcome my fears

When it seems like all the darkness

Is trying to drag me under.

18

There is no perfect way to be wise

Only learning and experience leading the way

The only way to get there is to take one step at a time

And make the most of every moment

Wisdom comes with age and sometimes it's hard to find

But it's always worth the journey, it brings happiness and joy

So don't be afraid to reach for wisdom, it's yours to claim.

19

Knowledge is power inscribed in the mind.

It can be used to make us rulers of our destiny.

Or it can be used to hold us captive in our own hearts.

Both are traps we can fall into if we're not careful.

But wisdom is also a light that guides us home.

Made in the USA
Monee, IL
07 July 2026